Reaction Time of Glass

James Peake was born in Wimbledon and educated at Bristol University and Trinity College, Dublin. He has worked in trade publishing for several years, predominantly for Penguin Random House and Pan Macmillan as well as independents and leading literary agencies. He lives in London with his wife and son.

Also by Two Rivers Poets

David Attwooll, *The Sound Ladder* (2015)
Kate Behrens, *The Beholder* (2012)
Kate Behrens, *Man with Bombe Alaska* (2016)
Kate Behrens, *Penumbra* (2019)
Adrian Blamires & Peter Robinson (eds.), *The Arts of Peace* (2014)
David Cooke, *A Murmuration* (2015)
Terry Cree, *Fruit* (2014)
Claire Dyer, *Eleven Rooms* (2013)
Claire Dyer, *Interference Effects* (2016)
John Froy, *Sandpaper & Seahorses* (2018)
A. F. Harrold, *The Point of Inconvenience* (2013)
Maria Teresa Horta, *Point of Honour* translated by Lesley Saunders (2019)
Ian House, *Nothing's Lost* (2014)
Gill Learner, *Chill Factor* (2016)
Sue Leigh, *Chosen Hill* (2018)
Becci Louise, *Octopus Medicine* (2017)
Mairi MacInnes, *Amazing Memories of Childhood, etc.* (2016)
Steven Matthews, *On Magnetism* (2017)
Henri Michaux, *Storms under the Skin* translated by Jane Draycott (2017)
Tom Phillips, *Recreation Ground* (2012)
John Pilling & Peter Robinson (eds.), *The Rilke of Ruth Speirs:*
New Poems, Duino Elegies, Sonnets to Orpheus & Others (2015)
Peter Robinson, *Foreigners, Drunks and Babies: Eleven Stories* (2013)
Peter Robinson, *The Constitutionals: A Fiction* (2019)
Lesley Saunders, *Cloud Camera* (2012)
Lesley Saunders, *Nominy-Dominy* (2018)
Jack Thacker, *Handling* (2018)
Susan Utting, *Fair's Fair* (2012)
Susan Utting, *Half the Human Race* (2017)
Jean Watkins, *Scrimshaw* (2013)
Jean Watkins, *Precarious Lives* (2018)

Reaction Time of Glass

James Peake

First published in the UK in 2019 by Two Rivers Press
7 Denmark Road, Reading RG1 5PA.
www.tworiverspress.com

ISBN 978-1-909747-51-7

1 2 3 4 5 6 7 8 9

Two Rivers Press is represented in the UK by Inpress Ltd
and distributed by NBNi.

Cover illustration by Sally Castle
Text and cover design by Nadja Guggi and typeset in Janson and Parisine

Printed and bound in Great Britain by Imprint Digital, Exeter

Acknowledgements

My thanks are due to the editors of the following, where some of these poems, or versions of them, first appeared: *The Next Review*, *The Inflectionist Review*, Eyewear's *Best of New British and Irish Poets 2017*, *Scintilla* and *Wild Court*.

I would also like to thank Ben McGuire, Roy Robins, Simon Willis and Peter Robinson for their advice and support.

For Kate

Contents

II.

I.

Storm

The only storm we'd ever seen whole,
as still as a building, waiting.

A solid hour yet to the outermost rains
almost coy with restraint when we met them.

The dark adjusted us
like the dark of an aquarium.

Nudging play in the steering wheel,
the radio snuffed and our fragile interior

no quieter. I retired the wipers
beneath a tonnage of suspended water

rife with schools of shadow
like a hundred harmonious species.

Birchwood

Remote holiday home, more rain threatening,
a weekend let tidiness, shadowy ceilings throughout,
showroom sofa and rug, a fallen cushion, and ourselves
liberated into animals, having followed the many trails
to these now ownerless clothes and toppled shoes.
We've been slow to notice the bare wood luminesce
as though in sympathy with the birches outside,
sisters at the glass, rooted and restless as tongues.

Anselm Kiefer

What is most real is destroyed
when you bring words, so bury
this painting, busy the canvas
beneath comprehending snow,
let open a latent orange
like the turn of an early tree,
a subterranean ceiling
is replete when pierced,
slanted rods of noonday sun,
the dust of southern France.

The Gift

My connecting flight is delayed
and the steady radar,
the bulbs on permanent red,
serve a city I've never seen in daylight,
a city through which the newly dead commute.

Like them I outstay.
Like them I don't know or notice.

You lived here with your husband
and loved me at a distance.

You complained because he read your messages.
Your marriage aged and you didn't.

The dressing gown in the guest room
was yours. While I waited for sleep
the shine told me wakeful things,
smoothness, travel, the impossible.

The front door in the night was my gift.

Dark Star

The road you touch with your wheels is endless,
another's daydream, the stranger aimed
at a receding horizon, afloat with boredom,

where you and he pass a quartered nowhere,
four mock-ups in need of both depth and colour,
you summon rain for those or a time-lapsed brake light
since both are weightless and spare as a thought

for the files and orts ghosting through you,
the dark star of appetite, glare and recognition,
the utter reality of other people,
those few you're able to acknowledge.

Colour, 1

It's not white noise but a space
inside which any human voice
can retune, regender, resurrect,
since the dead or the changed
are summoned by wax cylinder
or vinyl as it ingratiates the needle,
pops and clicks, an alive mouth
at my shoulder, there and not there.

The Heartbeat

Forgot I'd almost halved the sash when we got in
and now there's overnight rain
spattering the ginnel, our bins and the stoop,
making the empty street audible.

I should get up – gooseflesh in the dark –
but instead bring the duvet to your shoulder
as though to preserve us at our most gentle,
wordless, spent, soon-to-be-restless.

Are you awake, sweetie, or enough
for my lub-dub to coax that drifting mind of yours
somewhere it's never been, one image or a series
accidentally authored by me, my heart,

and there'll be birdsong and rain on the carpet
when we wake, as every morning, apart?

Cy Twombly

1

We saw your paintings, Cy,
the retrospective in Paris,
your name ablaze on the drop-
down banner on the Pompidou.
I don't know if you get used to that
or have to think, *he's someone else.*
We met men with rings of souvenirs
on each arm, and clothes racks in the street,
an empty whitewashed shop front
which, so long as it floats like that,
is infinite. It won't float for long.
I thought of the gallery *interregnum* –
does it darken like a theatre? –
readying for piercing yellows,
the apricots and private reds,
paint driven downwards
by your overloaded sponge
and the written out, rewritten names
released from antiquity
like guests who won't leave
and won't introduce themselves.

2

A warship
with vertical oars

is nowhere,
a dustless shelf,

Lexington, Lepanto,
Salamis, New Hampshire,

a second ship
implying others,

this harbinger bright
as a skull

with oars like driven pins,
a fetish

in cryptogenic light.

Performed in Total Darkness

Do you ever think about that pitch-black production of *War Music*?
The actors were guided round space, audience and each other
by a thoroughly wired perimeter, lengths taped to the floor,
in parallel, overlapping in air, knotted, tagged with bows
for a language extinct that very night, the run's close.
We woke to that nightmarish cradle when house lights,
for applause and the quantum return, came on.

There was achievement keeping it so dark so long,
and us in the poet's anachronistic, love-or-leave-it Troy,
our minds from alternative evenings. A fleeting car horn
and Ajax or someone tried to quiet his breathing.
Don't fight it, I thought, that makes it worse and even heroes
or villains run out of puff, weakness is not untrue,
there'd have been gasping and wheezing aplenty. Hamlet
at the Union, dead but not gone, was all nostrils and shut lips,
enacting the play-old problem, the nuisance of breath
in that laid-out tragedian, stillness needed the wrong end
of a vigorous fight scene. You saw someone drop for real.
They really drop dead, you said, the phrase says it all.

But back to the dark, with a laundry basket chariot,
worked and misshapen for an authentic wicker squeak,
coconut shell – what else? – for horses, and metal for metal,
mashers, maybe, spoons and pans, Ikea for Ilium,
and lettuce, the hands got through a mountain
for the way of all flesh, or flesh as it fares between armies.

They denied it, but I'm sure – the last night, remember –
they shot a real enough arrow over the front row,
I can feel it on my hair even now.

The Middle Places

Silence can be fierce or expensive, a place
from which opposites confirm us
like the polished glass and the metal behind.

I love it when you relax with your legs across me.
It's easier to tune in to what you mean
when there's touch, when there's no between.

Something interior gurgles with health
and you prod yourself and laugh.
The TV watches us when it's off.

Il Padre

After Fellini's 8½

Marcello calls after
his reappeared father.

He wants him to pause
and extend this chance

to add to what he knows of his father,
to what his father knows of him.

His father is dapper and no older.
Their ages are closer.

The dead man is a gift,
the flash of a mirror

into a deadened commute.
We hardly talked.

When Marcello straightens again,
he is no man's son.

The Motel

The forecourt sticky with repairs
and a sheltered Coke machine's

the strongest light.
While you pretend to sleep

I offer tomorrow's map
but see only the shadows of my fingers.

The letterbox button has slipped
and on the third or fourth attempt

it begrudges me a can
too cold to enjoy,

printed with the old design.

A Ruin

The interior uninscribed and without colour,
no characters or marks, the architect and his or her
builders became their opus so we don't know
fitting from votive, can't say what ornament
stood where or why this courtyard was kept clear,
lichen on its southern face like a Rorschach test
before such horizontal diagnostics could exist.
But the staircase we do get, both ways continue
to break down emptiness, deposit the curious
higher or lower according to personal whim
and no forgotten scheme where up is as well as down,
the price of admission a mask of inhuman design,
visitant within the painted eyes of a dolphin,
creatures not seen first hand but heard described.

Delphine

1

The dripping buildings speak to one another
in a language too young to decipher.

2

When we brought our bodies together for the first time
your breasts were cold from the afternoon rain.

Enough is Enough

1

As it grows the brain becomes smaller.
Lone against the sky, a stairwell is taller.

2

You're kind when confident, in pieces when cruel.
Selfhood is a knot in the flow of the usual.

3

The mass-produced and the private are the same,
a mitten on railings for no one to reclaim.

The Eye in the Wall

I've torn open too much plastic, tonnage
of cans and glass and their contents,
the petrol burned off to push me in my seat into the air,
the coins I've kept or dropped in callused hands,
the slow-grown shapes of animal and vegetable
I've pulped in my hunger, the body of water I've passed,
the insects squashed in hotel rooms and the gallon of anonymous
  blood
they gave up, the oxygen, the terrible things I've said and don't
  remember
but know the wounded must, entire songs rising from tarmac
I never bothered to admit, now gone, or re-gifted,
I go blank and clear with the weight, the grief,
ongoing in its having-been
until something, the early stars of a storm on parched grass,
the need to cough from histamine, the darkened sky shrinking
  the house,
the hurry of water as you top up your squash, is new, a first,
and I notice the fractional adjustments
keeping me steady, rooted, here,
the countless muscles in my face letting you know
that I see you too, and everything behind you.

Marine Snow, Hammersmith

The flyover this late is less than human,
the only evident affection
drops from the sodium vapours overhead
to the blue ruins they invigilate.

Hereabouts so exquisitely drowned
that nothing seems altered or sways,
glass doesn't cloud or give, and no one thing
self-seeks like submarine oxyacetylene.

My home is identical but not the same.
I squeeze irrelevant keys, taste familiar dark
unstirred by loved ones, my wife,
our child, ablaze with sleep. The shadows
of unseen fish dislodge from the roof.

II.

Gates of the Medina

I like being told where samples come from, cherish the urgency
in an actor's voice from film, that distant from normal speech
in clarity, patience and pith. Some designers exclude anything
a character wouldn't hear, they ditch the swelling orchestra,
the xylophone that signals Asia. Wooden voice. Metal voice.
Listened to my voicemail once on your phone. The prick. Why put
up with him? The sarcasm. Silence. Where was his mind always
wanting to go? And who with when it did? Apart from you.
Vast distance between a face and the smaller eyes behind it.
That one-off night I panicked and ran by torchlight, an app,
a preload. What does alcohol provide? The chance to condescend
or arise, as required. Hence we met. I can summon to mind
the Moroccan sunset but nothing of how our inclusion felt.
  Or did I think
our souls might be real and touched? I don't know where you
  live now,
your routine, wardrobe. You don't always keep to yourself as
  you vowed,
travel somehow when the house is asleep and respective partners
can't suspect. You speak coincidence, things met again, guiding
my cursor, rearranging text in the articles I scroll. We're like
children who improvise in sync, relegate the adults by example.

Two Coins

The coins we found
were unfamiliar,

their size, weight,
insignia.

We glued one to the floor
and the volume rose,

eyed the other
and the sun froze.

The Upstairs Neighbour

1

Touching food is like touching a chess piece
and means you're by code committed.

2

He thinks better of a sandwich assembled
forty miles away in the dead of last night.

3

None praise it now but he pushes the spoon
like an Edwardian, in the direction of childhood.

4

London's ovens are never cold.
It was the very hungry who made God remote.

Figure

Marble allows the light
beneath its surface,

an affinity with skin
bringing presence

and the impression
of pause, not stasis.

The audio claims
what is edited

remains,
that eliminated space

has weight,
attendant and mute,

as when a bed sheet
slipped, your down

stood,
I was erased.

The Weight

A figure they cannot name with confidence
holds something upwards and away from her breast,
her leftmost arm is emphatic, locked
at the elbow, concluded at the wrist.

She doesn't need eyes to show us fear
or the blossoming skull of a constrictor,
those hypodermic teeth or the smell of meat.

As if seawater has leeched the marble
she whitens as we stare, the impossible muscular
tremble – *there* – which makes the threat
and the weight and the ugliness real.

Carrion

We slouch beneath halogen bulbs
and they flow with rings like banded snakes,
one able to glide through walls,
one bringing change like a hormone.

We pass hardboard propped in darkness
and it breaks into distinct life,
down to the kerb, and from a nearside arch
eyes swallow us and go out.

On a bartizan turret, above the rain,
like the glory of Central Station,
is a bird of plumage and bulk,
the electronic cry of a virtuoso.

Your face is a stone laid over insects.
This close I hear the substrate,
how vast armies communicate.
Animals have entered the city.

Leviathan

Zoom out until the city is mute
and the skyline fits the viewfinder:

the uneven remains of a fluent monster
coaxed into shallows where it drowned,

teeming in the time-lapse,
glittering with nutrients.

White Clay

The maintenance trench
is length and width
a roadside grave,
filled overnight
with inbound water.

A corrugated eye
on the surface
confirms
the breach is live

and the harrowed walls
seem baked into place
by the sheer
and topped-up weight.

Like the refreshed sink
of a potter or butcher,
filling as much as draining,
level and high, holding clear
the clotted instruments,
dark-handled
with experience.

Plaything

So the only thing fixed is the brainless grin and
by letting anchoring wires groan and give
the lone figure can relax to the point of collapse
the way chloral hydrate overwhelms,
a buckled ankle, the headfirst dive to the floor.
But tension demands release one way or another,
things could go back, be as they were,
a heartbeat ago.

A heartbeat ago
things could go back, be as they were.
But tension demands release one way or another,
a buckled ankle, the headfirst dive to the floor,
the way chloral hydrate overwhelms.
A lone figure can relax to the point of collapse
by letting anchoring wires groan and give
so the only thing fixed is the brainless grin.

Herbertstraße

Anna's father has no fixed abode.
She couldn't find him if she tried.
Trust her!

And we do. We open up
before, after, instead.
She hides boredom like no one.

We make way for a woman carrying down
three black teas.

Anna paces herself better than I could.
The shift is 8 to 4. Tobacco, a little coke,
no alcohol.

From nowhere
we're talking fear,
the real draught,

a father and daughter
reunited
in ignorance.

She remembers a gentle voice.
Like an Irish broadcaster!
Little else.

Justified verse on her bicep.
She ignores the compliment,
asks what I want.

The Skin of Epimenides

Read *The Seven Sages* and you're asked to believe
this loner cured all Athens of disease,

backwards prophet who saw past not future,
first things first, like the irruption of order

into cosmos. But a seer doesn't want for time
and is free to pen nothing in yours or my lifetime.

There was an ageless stint in a cave, fifty-seven
years until, out of sync with prevailing fashion,

he flashed scars like the aftermath of disease,
a real enough itch he was unable to relieve

by pinching (from an ox-hoof) a greyish powder
of diminishing bliss, of sustaining disorder.

The scars were harmless, tattoos in foreign fashion,
self-inflicted glyphs numbering fifty-seven.

Sparta, none-the-wiser, flayed him for the future
to fathom like a drum skin, test to a powder.

The Retelling

Recycled air lifts your fringe and sets it down
as mine, our one face waiting for the southbound.

The cars pitched further along are empty
and the one which aligns opens and smells of hair.

That rapid sound so the doors know to close,
then brought up to speed, the loud silence of tunnel.

The return of steadier light allows her:
an elderly woman too small for her clothes,

lowered head and cumbersome hands,
a Londis bag whitened from reuse.

She is no one we know. One of her eyes
is the slower to close, and that's all.

The New Elite

Indemnity. Damnation. Limited Liability.
Bringing the rivers of hidden skulls
are the Bakerloo, Northern, Hammersmith
and City, six hundred bus routes, sponsored
cycles and swollen pavements,
the names such a flow upholds,

logos rotate, fill with light, drain,
console incomers from the airport
or in tunnels, a joint and several dream,
the names to which names attach,
like upturned cards on a CV's baize
or deactivated pass I found in a drawer,
my cheeks fuller, landfill suit and tie
for a thousand days I can't now distinguish,

a T junction wired for emissions,
this traffic island answering back
as an egg, buoyant with albumen,
and I make not judge a pause in traffic
and think, *surely this is not the place* (stepping off),
you can argue margins until you're blue in the face,
a plastic bag lifts and swoons like an animal
into the grill of an oncoming Fiat or Vauxhall.

The names to which names attach,
newborn, executor, maiden, saint,
how mistakes are repeated into truth
like an uncorrected imprint page
or my father's last and watched-for breath.

The Visitor

Your hand fell from the bed. You slept.
But I listened hard for a long time:

one of the stairs, the landing.
Someone had tried and failed the lock.

I did the rounds when I truly heard nothing
and granted the role of would-be intruder

to the stilled man I saw from our bathroom,
framed by the gates to the luxury site,

in front of ramps, mesh and grey liquid,
tilting his head

as though the better to hear
a single thing through a blueprint wall.

Colour, 2

It's not white noise,
the rush hour burr

raised by a suitcase,
overruled by a whistle

in an unknown language.
An empty station

will always arrive
at an equal silence.

The Club

Time is what things take
and a short set
of mirrored stairs
is enough to boundary
this world and another.

The club smells of cola
and the shoeless dancer
dances to her own reflection,
slower in the glass
by a telltale fraction.

Burin for an Open Hand

Stretch of adland emptiness
and westward from the flyover

buildings begin to shrink, wet
as the teeth in any jawbone.

I overtake my own sideways glimpse,
a lag of the senses

so that yards from where a terrace ends
I see the unchanged mural there darken,

its atmosphere of negative,
of cancellation, spreading like a film

across glass, metal or acetate,
as if to hide colour from a burin

till it scratches down, digs or nicks
the randomised palette beneath

and let stream the glow and afterglow
of a high street, the red, blue, green and yellow

of airless retail, Trade Marks and brands,
a jumble presenting as designed whole,

the last basis for things appearing as they do
on the change-down descent to street level,

level of the human, a sudden pedestrian
within arm's reach of the passenger seat

and who glides as though drawn by thread,
one I recognise, have held myself

inside a labyrinth with no secret,
heightened friends at every exit,

eyes-within-eyes
or an ideogram for a face,

if only I could draw or paint!
As I vanish back up into third,

cross an out-of-hours bus lane,
I remember or have somewhere just seen

a man in a branded cap (Just Do It!),
the dry plastic hand in his lap

holding to the shape of likelihood.

Two Rivers Press has been publishing in and about Reading
since 1994. Founded by the artist Peter Hay (1951–2003),
the press continues to delight readers, local and further afield,
with its varied list of individually designed,
thought-provoking books.

Two Rivers Press has been publishing in and about Reading
since 1994. Founded by the artist Peter Hay (1951–2003),
the press continues to delight readers, local and further afield,
with its varied list of individually designed,
thought-provoking books.